A SHORT HISTORY

OF FORGETTING

For Linda & Jim
Best wishes

Salt Spring Island
2016

A SHORT HISTORY OF FORGETTING

PAUL TYLER

GASPEREAU PRESS MMX

for my parents, and for Jacquie

We look at the world once, in childhood.
The rest is memory.
LOUISE GLUCK

Naming the Animals

ADAM NAMING THE ANIMALS

I

Speechless, clay between his fingers, he wandered
through woods where they darted and burrowed.

You must name them, the voice urged.

The man gestured to each animal,
watched their differences flickering.

But the voice said name them.

He gathered blossoms to wreathe their nests,
made piles of rocks where they had stood,

but still the voice said name them.

He tamed an ember left by a storm,
smoked the scrub to reveal their shapes.

Name them, said the voice.

He cleaved stone, flaked its edges,
caught them to bleed and butcher.

Almost, said the voice. Now name them.

The man, feeling something sever
within him, howled, to shut out the voice.

Good, said the voice. Name them.

II

They would not fit inside his mouth.

Cries bolted shut.
Ohs fell from his throat.

His tongue, feeling its corners,
searched under itself for explanations.

He needed sound with barbs—
something to still them:

they squirmed and flashed
in the leaves, ringing, he thought,

like bones hung in the branches.

III

He learned to see time outlined
in yellow on the hills, burning

the edges of his hands. He saw
creatures wander away alone,

dissolve into dirt. This is
who you are, said the voice.

Sizing a print, its flanges
blooming in the mud, he followed

tracks to a cave, heard
padded feet leaving its mouth.

He entered the dark pout,
tasted the air as he painted

handfuls of earth on the walls.
A fur-covered utterance

brushed his leg, and he
learned the hunger of vowels.

IV

The vertebrate crack of
stone to marrow
fed him. The end-snap,

glottal stop, scared him.
The interdental
throttle-sound, opening

the vowel in his gut,
sated him.
Bilabial hum, its quick,

knowing roundness,
sweet on the
tongue, woke him

to the crunch of speech.

V

The voice moved over the man while he slept.
It curled around his arms,

caressed his lips and throat,
slid across his skin, entered his ear,

whispered until the man's body
was nothing but a shape the tongue makes

with breath. When he woke, his flesh
mumbled; what he touched ached

for a word. The voice sprang
from his mouth, a flame of sound,

and the land lit; bones tugged
at their cage, leaves flashed on limbs,

small signals of themselves, pulling away—
the man terrified to open his mouth again.

VI

The voice returned and found him
shivering near a creek,
consonants knotted in his throat.

It clothed him in a hush, asking,
Would you rather be water? Perhaps stone?
Something carried lightly by wind?

The man gathered his words,
unfolded them from his lungs.

Make me music, a song hurtling from the bush.

But they fell against silence.

In the woods, with a sound like rain,
the animals leapt away.

IN PRAISE OF THE BANANA SLUG

Galiano Island, B.C.

Rain trips off blackberry leaves, quick cloud-lettings
let slugs slip out, rippling all over, cruising
(oh yes, cruising) wooden beams,
slick oil-skinned sea captains.
In the drizzled sheen the whole yard
jiggles like an organ donor clinic.
Big moss-breakers, branch-snappers,
sloppy in the leaves, bush-busters
pushing up the porch—here's one
scripting toward my foot. Messy end
of evolution, overnight whole-zucchini inhaling lung,
don't mistake my toes for snap peas—
though I deserve it, stomping, stabbing, pouring salt coats.
Amends! Take my garden!
Lucky my rubber-booted neighbour is gone,
grim-faced in her slug-jig. Who could step on you?
Thick inches of earthen jelly, long as my foot,
heavily-spotted gummy glutton stretching up from the Cambrian.
Anything that patient, dragging its long ass
through miles of rain-worn woods
without picking up a sliver has my full attention. Go,
hungry puddle of nerves, gobble
the earth's green gibberish, seek your leafy crevices,
your tender buds, slide back huge
through glistening hollows of shrub, heaving
your tug-o-war load below the gaze of gardeners.

CRICKETS

They rub out their name again and again,
miniature black jackets
rustling under lamps, expecting
important guests; they want you
to give up everything—little socialists.
Eventually you will. Not yet. For now,
moonlight enunciates your body;
you walk in the field through talking air.
Dark weaves of grass hum your legs
beside a thousand improbable events.
Their tiny hooked feet carry songs,
climb with you up narrow steps to dawn.

MIDGE

Slim second of living
juice. Loose thread
of life. Pin puncture
in the air's fabric,
which is joy. Succinct
buzz of all that is.
Indelible legs. Antennæ
made of speck. Vibrant
throb of dust on my
wrist's bristle, which is
the reverberated hum
of the beginning,
which is all that ever was.

SILVERFISH

A silver lick along the crevice
filth, exploits the tile's wealth.
Vulgar lunge of tongue. Thin
peel of celestial refuse. A flat
note fallen off a sloppy angel's
lute. Flute-bug. Staccato e e e
(up a sleeve) xylophoning bone.
Or a dangled gala jewel. Regal
worm. Such a bitty itch-fish, tub-
crabbed in a drain. Embedded
peek-a-boo lining a grout-crack.
Scurried impropriety, gulped into
a squirm-hole. Co-evolved wiggler.
Dusty mirrored shimmer-shadow
in the house flesh, nibbling excess.

A PRACTICAL APPLICATION FOR BEES

Discussing their dancing, their miraculous wiggles, the biologist reveals how they measure distance to flower, calculate weight—two wags to the left, one complete turn, meaning, just over the hill there's clover. Their pantomime maps performed in sweet air, retraced by his details and charts. A little envious of bees, perhaps, he weighs his research in units of honey, waits in the wings for their succulent reply. O poet of apian data, pedagogue of the marvelous comb—go ahead, preach the sticky esoterica of bee philosophy, enact their sobering hum in our mind's hive, savour the pleasure of their kneeling labour. Breeding deep in the manna of hope, they propagate a ceaseless ethic of one for all. When asked to justify his fieldwork, our eyes swarm to him; his words seek the pollen of our favour. He allows evidence to amplify their hover through chart and diagram: show how a worker's slingshot trajectory, maneuvered by desire, captured by model and graph, assists advanced medical procedures. Sweet apiologist absolution. And let's not forget the military. Bee systems incorporated into robots, unmanned vehicles buzzing Baghdad with bombs on bee technology. O holy holy holy holy bee, facilitating our way of life with your benevolence, your selfless ardour, lubricating the machinations of our cogs with your magnanimous buzz.

WINTER CHICKADEE OFFERING

Propeller-winged feather-berries, icy air-rustlers,
pecking at this, at that, like my fingernail—
don't take that. Their tiny eyes, black dots
of fear. I say go ahead, go ahead, my jutted
hand a bird-plate. Come on down from there.
As if nerve-brains could fit anything snappier
than a seed. My words no more than chirps,
anyway. Their painful needle-beaks jab, pinch
my frozen digits; they don't care. Hurry up,
I say, ungloved for their ease, waiting for the
last fluttered blackcap chased away by old hens
of this seed-filch. He circles up, over, clings,
feather-nipped, finally lands. A pinky-percher.
He just sits there. Thought-starved. My own
little finger bauble. Take the seed, you twit.
This hub-bub's overrated, my fingers prairie-
licked, numb-knuckled, my hands wind-pounded
into nerveless sacks of bone. But I wait. Say,
there you go, and he takes it, so I reglove, having
given of this broken nut to another bushed believer.

GOLDFINCH MISTAKEN
FOR A SWALLOWTAIL

It unfolds air like song,
but yellow.
A thin flutter between breaths

nesting in your seeing—oh
things began,
you think, in golden wonder.

Someone ahead on the path
invents it: "there—
a butterfly," its quick flash, faster

than thought, brightly punctuated.
You piece together
a lean-to of reason, suggest

"a bird, I think," but too late,
the little nova
of awareness gone, its burning thread

tied to memory, flaming down
dark tunnels of words,
the afterglow, bright believing.

HOUSE SPARROWS

Thin chippers, white bread doodlers,
little humdingers—
froth-whipped mobs of bugged-up
feathers, wire-creep
for evening shots at eave lips.
Roof litter, hived in heaps,
house clackers, vent jammers,
tossed together in rubbish
tangles. With quick eye-bits
they spot loose nibbles,
crave a crud-fix. Crumb leeches.
Wind thrips, preening
in dirt pits with snail-slicked
beaks. Junk-snapping
wrapper addicts, hop-busking
for scrap. One-note
wonders, bland survivors,
riffs on a street-grub origin of species.

HUNGRY

I'm howled awake; his claws flex, scrape
under the door, his unreadable mouth
releasing insistent vowels. Tail perked,
he runs to the kitchen, as if everything
is simple: the air we breathe, our hunger.
And after, he sits close, washing night
from his face, the agreement fulfilled.
Other mornings a more complicated
scramble rakes the floors—soft wings
slap against glass. A rabbit he caught,
screaming under the bed. A mourning
dove, crouched exhausted on the sill,
a growing bead of blood escaping its
skull. I gather these gifts into boxes,
let them bring themselves back or cease.
If I pause in my betrayal, prying one
still alive with fear from his perfect jaws,
I can't bear his look of confusion;
it's almost too much, I almost give in.
What we love, we love. The thing that
illuminates him, aims him, I can almost
touch it: its brightness flaring in his mouth.

PIG

Struck, drooped, dead. Rolled in cold on a skid.
Forklifted up and dropped for the butcher, who
greets it like a patient. He kneels in, pinches its
jowls, slaps its flank, pokes the bloated tongue,
heads for a bucket, happy. The pork-hunk waits
on ice for knives. Its throat a flabby slit all bled.
Humourless pile of meat. The stiff-gazed charm
pulls the room's glances. A strutting stock boy
delivers a kick to its gut, peels a smoke, pops it
up the snout: puff on that. A circle of chucklers
gathers until the butcher gumboots back, howls,
swears: *that's the face of my ex*. He's got other
bones to break, blood to wash back, so leaves it
draining in its goblet of dark, its muscle-fix, its
hair-joints, skin-chops, its smile that won't thaw.

WINTER MOOSE, ALASKA

Walking the roadside skim of trees, deep
Fahrenheit blurring my lungs, I stop
between skidoo veins, see prints
pounded in snow. As if darkness
thought *moose*, it slaps out, a bull,
new bulbed rack with powder flaring off.

I slide back stupid, breath on the stars,
as a glow crests the hill: a quad gnawing
toward us, yanking a swerving sled
of boys, oblivious. The moose bolts
through frozen tangles, becomes
a clod of dark again, night scribbling-in.

An hour later, walking back, I spot a Chevy
squatting there, steaming—windshield
webbed, its grill smashed, flagged red
with moose hair. *We were lucky,* he says,
hand resting on the wheel, headlights
sleeving the birches while he waits for a tow.

LAST POLAR BEAR

Stanley Park Zoo, Vancouver 1996

Old shag body shelved on a slab of concrete.
December rants against his yellowed burden.
Soon to be shipped, sold, not much bear
anymore. People circle, embarrassed, moving on.
Downpour opaque, gutters slurp, choke.
Cars jerk down streets like damaged cells.
Beyond that, a rough-skinned drum of inlet.
Vines of suburbia creeping up mountains.
A northern spine of snowcaps carrying the sky
where ice hints over rivers—brittle ideas
partly formed. The season's attention, thin.
At the centre, buried in a bruise of cloud, his
cold dream slows under sheets of iceless light.

Short Histories

A SHORT HISTORY OF FORGETTING

for Paul and Kathy

Loading their jumbled, last bags—friends, neighbours, leaving this city—
we accept pieces of the disorder, the placeless piled around their car,
things that wouldn't fit, couldn't be tossed, hard evidence of being here.
Slumped in long coats, we watch them dig through cupboards,
hold up offerings, dislodge the belongings stuck so long in corners
they'd grown roots, things taken as if from themselves, no longer
recognizable. Everything rises to the surface, exposed, refusing the
order of boxes, lives distilled from time. The mats, faded lids, saucers.
The never-repaired hunks of things, slabs of wood, the wire, broken
bits of us unexplained, spelled out on the floor like coordinates to
a place overgrown, unreachable, signifying only a habit of keeping.
They slip the key under the door, offer quick goodbyes, last waves
in November wind as we watch them drive down the one-way street.
Carrying the weight for them to the dumpsters, we place it hesitant
into darkness, then climb back into ourselves, falling asleep, weightless.
The next morning I hear it shift, see the boxes of clutter strewn around
the alley. That man, I forgot, is here every week, and he lifts through
it like debris after a disaster. His expert hands test the heft of wood,
set aside what can be sold, used: a threadbare shirt raised to the light,
a squeaky answering machine that held my voice—it feels like robbery,
but he knows the line between stealing and archeology, walks beautifully
among the ruins of belonging. Taking the past apart from the inside,
he dismantles the ghost apartment—broken cups, a shattered clock, things
to patch together on the other side. From here it's easy to see the border
between memory and history; everything is forgotten, and resurfaces
in another's hands. He stuffs that bag, his life, walks away hard with it.

SHORT HISTORY OF A WEDDING PHOTO

Café Hon, Baltimore

Nailed there. Frame dented. Greased above the grill.
Café trinket hung up slanted. Near the Coca-Cola clock

ticking beyond the bride's banded finger. White dress
blooms in her hand. She's not sure where to put it all.

Groom, tux-pruned, leans sideways—can't quite
see her anymore. Shy lips in half-smiles, uncertain.

So they should be. How to cut cake four-handed.
Which car to take. Who will drive them to the hall

of anonymity to kiss on demand. More like immigrants
than newlyweds. Stunned. Just off the plane. First steps

in a chaotic land of plenty. Thirty years I'd guess. Warped
by steam. Dimmed with dust. Endless mornings of regulars

assuming significance. Though no one working here
knows them. Ritual dwindles to superstition, kitsch.

Like a cabbie's dangling rear-view Virgin. A great aunt's
mounted Pope plate. Visitors look up, get a jolt of nostalgia.

Appetite. Exchange mystery for unambiguous narrative.
What survives such casual glancing? They carry on

despite everything, all smiles and orchids. Faces glowing
like old light bulbs, blazing through the generational haze.

Caught at the blurred edge of the camera's imperfect
aim, some keep-to-himself cousin, not so much ignored

as forgotten, who showed up anyway, too early, drunk,
slurring at the bar, smudges the corner of the photo. Abandon—

always closer than we guess. Yet like a window, permanent,
no one yanks them down. No one even touches them.

THE FATHERS ARE DYING

for Brier

The quiet in their eyes. Long stares through kitchen windows.
Ball caps, old jeans worn on Sundays.
Waking at odd hours, papers by their chairs
rearranged the next morning.
Deep sighs (in through the mouth, out through the nose)
whenever anyone asks a question.
Inscrutable gifts given to their children.
Unexpected laughter, inappropriate grins—
O undefinable fatherly glee.
Their great hope that at least one of their children
will excel at mathematics.
Watchtowers in the mind where they pace,
prophets of everything that gets worse.
Poor taste t-shirts and finger pulls.
Letter openers from Malaysia.
Old toys sealed in boxes you were never allowed to touch.
Waking you at four a.m. on a school night
because Venus is passing closer to Earth than it will
ever again in our lifetime, he says.
The fathers are dying, go and listen to them breathe.
Some have risen from their chairs to answer the door,
to check on the dog when it didn't return.
They are calling in the night and will not come home.
Some melt away into white sheets
seeking a sleep that is finally their own.
When they are gone, so are the tools,
the guidebooks and wood stoves,

the crossbeams, the nails, the O-rings and joists.
So are the maps, so is time, so is love
which you didn't expect. Once he is gone
the questions and the answers
remain locked in a trunk at the back of his den,
its quiet stickers from Milan and Salzburg,
its aroma of eucalyptus and sandalwood,
its stiff hinges, difficult latches, its mouth sealed with ash.

THE LIST OF WHAT WILL LAST

Nothing but a few hairs. And a pebble
you always kept in your coat pocket.
Your memory, changing, of love.
The green of woods at night, and
the gravel road that took you there.
Something about a ship in a song
you heard just once. A book
given to you by your grandfather
left unread in the rain. Thirst.
This will always matter. And pennies—
their irretrievable faces. The sand dollar
loose in your desk, unbroken,
despite all your leaving. The blink
of chance that brought us here
from tiny life in ocean pools.
The body, so frail, outliving the mind,
its million parts, reborn and reborn.
Gravediggers. Skulls of jesters and
hummingbirds. The patience of crows.
A glance from someone you love
who doesn't love you. A photograph
thought incinerated in the Blitz.
But not the stars (you hopeless romantic).
Nothing locked, or floated in a bottle on the sea
(you are lost now, admit it).
Not your first memory or your last,
and certainly not the list, though
someone might recognize a colour,
a rhythm, a scent, and it will
continue a little longer before it stops.

Of the twelve-storey twin buddhas, elaborations
of sandstone, cave-pocked hills, thousand-year
stares, eighty percent—the expert says—
has been blasted away by howitzer, explosives
drilled into torsos, detonation wires binding
desolate limbs. They're just rock, a blight
on God, the official insists—as if history,
left unwatched, simply grows giant buddhas
in forgotten deserts, vacant weight left in stone,
a civilization's quarry emptied. I get centuries
confused: torch-lit reformers razing Europe,
smashing alabaster belief; entire languages
cleansed, the burning mouths of millions.
Which twenty percent is left—a wind-torn thigh,
unmoving; the right hand in flight, its palm
clapping dirt near a clutch of armed men; knees
crumbling into myth, dogma invented from
dust; or an eye carted to a pit, buried, wide open?

SHORT HISTORY OF
FERDINAND VON ZEPPELIN'S DREAM

Exact in leather the airmen rode neat in hydrogen-bellied beasts,
rising through Europe's darkness, and into the Great War.
Von Zeppelin believed his machines, launched over fields
of sorrow, would spread black fire for the Kaiser, ignite
conflagrations of the weak, bring an early ending. Cordage
slapped in channel winds, a blind herd berthed from cloud.
London's walled gardens gulped down bombs, fat handshakes
of flame melting prams and milk bottles. The grey hides
circled, massive in the smolder, mechanical grinding churning
light. Cloth-winged biplanes chased, but the airships easily
rose, groping home along stars, trailing the cordite reek
of empty bomb bays, stirring search beams. For months
headlines greased *Huns Kill Babies;* streets became names
for fear. Until an ace released a phosphor splatter from his
overwing Lewis, its blue streak sinking deep into a bloated
gas cell. At first a finger of flame curled within the Zeppelin,
then like a hole poked in a star, night hemorrhaged, metal
flesh peeled back—twenty men, sudden sticks of light,
simply leapt. Cat walks, steel ribs, the whole molten mass
hovered, slid toward the Downs. London cheered below
death's lamp, the Zeppelin seeding sparks. Europe dug-in
beneath sorrow, its children sharpening the smallest of knives.

CANDLES IN THE SNOW

On the night they started bombing we lit candles in the snow
in snow the candles they started bombing on the night we lit
the candles they started on the snow we lit in night bombing
we the snow they lit on the bombing night started in candles
lit the snow bombing in the night started candles we on they
started in the night snow they on candles we lit bombing the
candles in the they we lit on snow the bombing started night
bombing night in lit snow candles started the we the they on
night snow bombing candles lit the we started on they in the
snow started night on the candles we lit the bombing they in
the night started in bombing snow we they on the lit candles
they lit in snow we on candles the night the bombing started

HOUSE SMASH

For Ken M.

Swallow-gutted, blank page of prairie windbreak, bottle-capped
drive, gravelled, greening. Not-here house, malice peeled to
bone, frightened reek of a wounded bird. Wide-eyed window
frames smashed open, acid tongues of poplar hiss rear in wind.
A sledgehammer night slugged it back down, gin-fisted kids
wet with youth splashed into walls. Old house, with drapes
leaking through, half-devoured, drop-kicked in this quiet copse.
Butt-ground steps and unspent shells loaded into earth around it.
Whatever passed through, moved on, exploded again in some
uncounted house from now. Dried paint-bucket lesions,
handprint language smeared in red. Broken cups and a magpie
roof, ripped, split with sun. This is how we fail the world.
Dragonfly-laced weeds offer purple comfort. A wide, blue
frame of sky, where walls lean on a shoulder of busted-up dream.

IF I WERE A PAINTER

I'd paint the dull brown mud—the canal duck-sludge in low water between seasons,
   the grey of this sky, and the concrete, its assurance of overcoming.
I'd paint plastic bottles kicked next to the curb, the drink lid in an overcast of leaves,
   cracks in the overpass, the cars pounding over, the black of faded asphalt.
I'd paint gravel collecting near grates, clogged with sticks, and across the studded
   grime, the nest of used spray cans under this dead, three-day rain-light,
the cold, swollen lawns, the page nines of newsprint, bellowed, wind-tortured near
   the wet glimmering benches. I'd paint bus stops, abused, broken-willed
shelters, hollow beside grass-invaded lots, the posters, limp, left hanging off poles.
   I'd paint this for all our dislocated gazes, for our half-intentioned lives.

THE PLAYERS

Baltimore, Maryland

Like abandoned buildings, the outfielders angle,
half-demolished in their bodies. Custom
thick as ivy keeps them here. Rookies
bow in dugouts, queue as if for confession.
Basemen punch gloves, shine in the diamond,
aim their blackened glances, rehearsing
distance. Cleats cut the earth. The shortstop
scuttles like a crab, scavenges a ball, sucks
it up in his glove, beams it to first with a force
his parents don't recognize. When the pitcher
rises to the mound, a balled-up blessing
masses his hand. Like a heron, sharp over water,
he waits for the twitch of sound—his name
insisted from stands—insatiably he splits the air.

THE SAD BAKER

Flour-thick light ignites a halo around him. *No bread!* he shouts, swishing us away, his roundness piling up basement steps. Hat a clump in his hand, he smears his face and softens: *maybe tomorrow.* Lamb pops on corner grills. We slip between whitewashed buildings, tired, tripping over cobblestone, wanting bread. I remember in the morning how the bed maker woke us. She waited by the door as we dressed in a rush. I touched your shoulder, still warm from sun spilt in the room. Packs heaved, we scrambled for the bus, seeking a shortcut, surprised to find the bakery again. I wanted mouthfuls of something quick, but the windows were boarded. A chain secured its door. It's been years now since I've even heard your voice, but waking this morning, I still see the baker. Wide with shadow, his lips fold into his face. His arms are heavy as salt. The street's aromas lift in the air, and I watch him wiggle powdered fingers beneath his apron, sink them into his heart.

To be lost in slow narratives, led uncertain through doors opening
onto doors, new masks for each scene—the body not a simple story,

she wants it told in full, and with good dialogue. Broken, he wants
flesh to become ritual; no longer instinctive, only ceremony raises

the flame, the *anima*. He cannot touch her—when inspired he needs
tools, objective distance, an intermediary. This Ur-myth of the body,

tale of original pleasure, orated in the mind's plush foyer—public
as hors d'oeuvres, splayed plums tempting hunger from demure

appetites—what matters shows. Revealing forgotten footpaths, they
seek glistening possibilities of an unplayed performance, an open-

air set. The chorus hides sweetly in the wings—the ghosts, pulleys,
the trap-door surprise. Gorgeously, they bow to the other's generous

roar, drenching applause strips them, absolves them of years bitterly
swallowed like stones: "brilliant," they weep. "It's so brilliant."

NEIGHBOUR

From a junk-vast room, its wine-stained stink,
stale bread counters, you pace into slippered
midnight's coalish dark—old-haired, low-
buttoned, wearing your past-the-expiry-date
ethos. Sidewalk smoker, bones blackened
with addiction, always a whisper for my cat
before backing down the hole of your life.
Wife, that old word, still itches your tongue;
you cough her name in clots behind tales
of a twenty-year office. In the heat-sunk,
after-five glow, thin-walled to mine, the pearled
voice of your favourite stranger does her job,
leaves you disappointed to absorb alone
the last warmth of this spilled-on, front-porch
day of days, my gentleman, my neighbour.
You rise when you see me, lifting from your
body's collapse to offer me the cheapest of reds.

VANITY HEARSE

So souped-up, only the hip get their final lift
in the back of this reconditioned soul delivery
machine. Its well of black, a fleshy embalmed
shine, could be adolescent audacity, the heavy
lick of chrome, painful. Its prowling promise
to outperform desire, hits a gear so glorious it
shifts you straight to godhead, your demeanor
the coolest it's ever been, a joke so deep inside
nobody gets it. With a Michelangelo baritone
idle, it aches to rev you out-of-here beautifully,
near liquid slant-six pumping angel wings for
plugs. On sweet holy-mag bliss, it rumbles off
to the legendary dead, low-riding over the Styx.

Urban Night Longing

ANTE MERIDIEM

Stars retreat up their sleeves;
the moon, in an alley,
sleeps under boxes.
Beneath maples, feeling
for the road, a car
gazes, almost seeing.
All over the city we rise;
our mouths are
pink flowers, opening.
Through corridors,
out doorways,
floating above our footsteps,
we listen to the wind
as it stiffens,
then climb onto its gurneys.

THIS BOOKISH NIGHT

You sleep like a comma in a thousand-page
dark. Moths flip loose around lamps.
Glowing paragraphs of high-storeyed
buildings anchor narratives of progress.
Rain chalks hymns on a hornbook lawn.
Fissures open an index of bats, dark
orders that bind us. Rereading dog-eared
alleys, sirens steer narrowly around you.
Stay a little longer, the story goes. Half-
read, you are stitched by possible endings.
There's that sound, repeated in your ear,
a crisp turning of hours; it keeps you here.

PIGEON FEATHER

Twist of city air, scoop of wind
oiled-up in an asphalt mud-dip.
Fallen tip of bliss, tobacco-pool
detritus in this parkade ecology,
preened off a grey-matter roost.
Huddled in a concrete acoustic
coo, O weak footed, wide-eyed
hydraulic-necked Pollocks, this
feather is a shot from the drum-
kit clap off of high-rise rooftops,
startled ovations so easily given.
Hillbilly peacocks, bent-beaked
with blues, you twang the single-
stringed call of pain. This oar to
the universe, ragged with tickle,
modest as a note from mummed
sheets of hymns. A barbed little
hand, placed in my hand, I hold
in my book of books to carry me.

THE HYACINTHS

The hyacinths sing, speared by stems
their open-mouthed yowl of blue
salutes the air; greedy little bankers,
they lunge at you with handshakes.
Under the sun, tight-belted, swaggering
like a hundred drunken Hemingways,
they wrap you in nectared caresses,
blast you with blunderbuss sorrow.
O the hyacinths, masters of ontology.
They Dietrich their way toward you,
press bee-swollen lips against your ear
humming smashed-heart melodies.
Perky old ninety-somethings, sipping
summer sherry from black thimbles of bliss.

TREE FAITH

Night-dimmed branches,
feathery,
weave into air.
Something crawls
around in you
as needles lisp with wind.
Bark musk clings
in the dark
limbs' harvest
of shadow; your
body curves
around a question.
High in their own
time, cones
click; wrapped
in green awareness,
the slow vein
beside you, pumping night.

MANITOBA MAPLES

Beaning from pavement moss, eyelets in walls, green-quivered
delicates spiked into asphalt morass, helpless, twig-legged.
Until their roots python, bulge into sewer veins, Godzilla-limbs
arching over rooftops. Opportunistic cuckoo trees, seeding
fund-pinched, zoned-to-be-condoized intersections, unnoticed
in the dumpster-moist dark and sprayed brick lairs, sprouting.
These halloween decorations gone feral loiter in disused lots
plotting chaos. Megalomaniac weeds, bug havens, bird bramble,
messed-up, misshapen bouffant heavies, more given names
than a nineteenth century Austrian countess. No one just says:
tree. Laid-back neighbours suddenly insist on shredders, buy
mid-life-crisis chainsaws. One maple, rumoured to have dropped
a branch on a widow's head, waited years for the right angle.
Another slipped a muddy claw inside a basement duct, opened
the house right up in a hemophilic spilling of oil and heartache.
Near a stumbling Manitoba town I saw some last-century hutch
stabbed up the middle by a young maple, pronged out windows,
deciduous mess of dust bowl bankruptcy. Could be your life next—
the neighbour points, eyeing up the grand trunk's indifference
to fence lines—could cause wires to snap, flatten your roses, a cat,
bring down satellite beams, screw with calls to old-world aunts,
nest in the driveway's winter heaves, spring through the Camaro
convalescent on blocks, stripping it to its chassis. See that crack?
Your foundation might be next. It'll creep inside while you sleep,
drop pods in your dreams, this shambling mound of uncompostable
leaves, this pollen puffing lawn-squid; it has nothing better to do.

A SHORT HISTORY OF OUR
FUTURE WITH THE ALIENS

On the day the aliens come, I'll still go into work;
it'll be all the talk at the office. It's getting closer.
What skills they'll bring from their foreign star.
What devices of pleasure. As they squat, posing
their ganglia beneath a strange blue sky, rubbing
their droopy eyelids like sleepy toddlers, asking:
Don't you know who we are? Of course, we'll cry,
we have heard all about you, offering the best of
our primitive hearts. As they slink from the haze
where the spacecraft sulks pulsing like a kidney,
their procession, with a sobering hush, will pass
through the burst of flashbulbs, metallic clothing
humming in its weave. They'll slide straight into
the mayor's congenial quarters, and be refreshed
with seltzer. This is the way it will happen. I'll be
at the office knowing everything has arrived at its
inevitable conclusion, and as silence descends like
a train depot at midnight, things will finally change.

CREATURE OF WORK

Office-frumped behind buttressed manuals,
preening folders of impotent numbers,
he perfects work's seamless equation:
know too much to be let go, do too little
to threaten. The economy's humble engine.
Sealed by the fan's thin lick, half-flesh,
half-fluorescent, his gaze bends corners,
his lamp casts prismatic cynicism. Neat
like a packet of aspartame tucked in a shirt,
he assesses shadows slouched at desks,
punctures distance with immaculate stride.
Forty hours of accurate motion, nothing
touches him. Rain arcs around him on his
cruel commute that never takes him home.
Stuffed in an outbox called weekend, cigarette
incinerating him, he recites names of those
who left, their faces flickering in discarded ash.

ABROAD

Out there—a wave of her hand—the unhere,
where everything is just so oh-well, so
beyond, you know? Been there twice,
once for good, returned only to leave again;
been there, and never the same. Truly, go.
No place like it. Living elsewhere, even better.
No more indecisive, place-bound trolling,
groping familiar terrain, ducks in a row—
shed it, lose it, drift away unattached.
Cultivate inner fields of frolic, golden apples.
Habit-breaking lands of nod will dash your
bugaboos. Suicide notes stuck up with
fruity fridge magnets? Forget it, scooter.
Just give me the stick. Plane-bound, no frills,
seas-a-plenty, chlorine tab, and my sweet
solo ass. Can't be bothered. No time
for legions of drear, those corked, bloated
beef-heads. Give 'em the fat one. Photocopy
your flipper and hit the turf. Listen, lightweight.
Time is short. Spend your eggs, drop your
tools. Give the monkey a slap. Who needs it?
And when you get back from out-of-here
your sad, entropic grin, your shovelled
face, will be a shining mirror of infinite places.

FIRST SNOW

The city oak just stands there, getting white,
hoping winter's first steps walk away,
stop bothering it. It has no idea. These damp
kisses don't care about love. These soft
shoes, made before sidewalks, before oaks,
aren't even shoes. They echo an original
ache so protean it can strip its silky hide,
dive into glacial streams of sky, shake
needling spray like a fly-mad musk ox,
burying the city under six feet of remorse.
It rakes on a broken violin at midnight
inside the porch, smashes the flower box,
cracks open autumn jukeboxes of birdsong,
spilling a starling's cackle and hiss, pissing
jet cold brew down chimneys. It drives
home without headlights like hammered
prairie teens after a piss-up, accelerates
through the garage door, again. Proto-poetic
provocateur. Mytho-generative cold snap.
Cronus eating his children. The shattered house
of Job. Kali beading her tether of skulls.
Poor oak. Its wretched, broken, leafless crown.

SPRINGSIDE AFTERPLOW

Grit-studded, once-white mound of inner winter.
Core of cold. Jackhammered by rain for weeks,
now calving mud-slushies. Dispossessed species
of snow. Growling, gravel-gutted, drippy heap.
Salt-lick pigeons circle-back and sucker-peck.
Garbage cups poke out like ears. Man-made
salty beast, basking hippo-like in crass puddles,
hunkered into rutting streets. Climate abscess.
Caustic death-scab slabbing the walk. City pocks.
Relentless February leftovers, belching into March.
Let go, street-sloucher. Return to stream. Flow.
Tire-thawed grin of dirt, leaching up skirt-hems.
Soaked-down gutter-sprawled bottle-grouch.
Mess of synthesized sludge. Ice dreck. Grime-fed
plow chaff. Old winter's bastard, humping the road.

A moaning, gin-soaked creaker aching in its shoes.
Wind-fists bang and bang to get in. Depth
charges pound around this deep-leagued explorer
of cold, this sub-zero house. Broken open,
a once-quiet street whips its arms, its iffy
wires, whistling switches of birch and oak.
Ice brittles, shrinks like a clerk. Foomp, foomp
and foomp, air stampedes the roof. Its shingles
rough as North Sea skin, a smashed-clam
face of a pious fisherman pulling a rope of prayer,
his catch of light a long, thin line leading
home through walls of ocean. Squall of illegible
longhand. An unhinged exuberance howled
by midnight-liquored boyos. Winter's white drink
scalds. Its grip, Saxon, berserks against civilized
eavestroughs, trim goes crooked in a beamed blur
of ice pellets, its burst blown from blistered lips,
lanes and alleys swinging off the flicker-to-black
grid—only a tiny hope of furnace, digging deep.

LAST SNOW

So brave the way it pretends nothing changes.
How it hopes. Its posture, soft against green,
reveals doubt it won't admit to, white shadow
along skinny arms of birch, where unformed
leaves wait in ambush. Its last, white rush like
Pickett's Charge: we can believe in desperate
acts, an hour of honesty with nothing beyond.
Rubbing snow's grief into our flesh, returning
warmth blazes it into oblivion, its final attempt
touching grey limbs, hissing: *you'll miss this,*
what might have been, had you wanted it more.

Home

DRESSING ARTHUR

When he won't let the night shift undress him
we find Arthur in the morning lost in a sweat,
mummified in heavy bedspreads, v-neck wiped
with dinner, wool trousers itching his tweezer
legs. Like a dream, unable to make his body
his own, he loads a fist, aimless in a slow swing:
phug uff he sputters as I strip the damp sheet.

T-shirt a second skin, it takes an hour to unbeam
his barricaded arms, to peel the layer from his
shrunken frame. We leave his light on all night;
so frightened of darkness, he won't even pull
his head through a tunnel of clothing. Tug too
hard, his grip tightens like a blood pressure strap
on limb or neck, obscenities unfurling from his gut.

Half-blind, he shuffles out at night, holding
his crotch. He cranes his small head, coughs:
whairs the tow'let? Glasses lost for weeks,
I scribble through his sight, lead him there,
a tin-man jerking beside me. Afraid he'll seek
the dark throat of stairs, I later wedge a chair
under the knob—for his own good (I tell his son).

Each morning, we shovel him out, take him ruffled
to the table, his eyes whirls of red. He is a slim
bone with tangled last divots of hair. Refusing his
bowl, he droops his head to a cup of wrinkled
hands, strains two words: *Sorry,* he says … *'m sorry.*

THE WORDS OF PHYLLIS

Words spill from her as she swats
the air. Visitors speak to the
side: *This isn't who she was—*
she used to be an actress.
Scripts, and snippets of songs
play through her, their shapes
perform on her lips; her tongue
deliberate as a finger on Braille
follows patterns that lead nowhere.
The aphasic storm of syntax
darkens her face, uncouples her
eyes from seeing. She retreats
to a room at the end of language,
its crumbling walls reveal her
spitting the gravel of her name.

GWEN ASKING THE TIME

Zimmer-sturdy, she's straight up,
mind jangled
with memories, last coins
in a tin: *I was a nurse, you know*
she scolds, cold toast
crumbling in her bitter mouth.

Sit down, eat your meal; she taps
her neighbour's plate
again; eyes flare over tea rims
then: *So much whining around here.*

She can't remember what she ate,
but knows it was awful,
the TV too loud, her tea too cold,
that someone slept in her
favourite chair, stole her sweater—
she knows misery, never asks to leave.

Each Sunday her sister
bundles her to church—
no one asks her name.
She sighs in the foyer,
points at the clock, knots
a scarf tight under Gwen's
chin: *Never make me wait.*

Gwen is never ready; we nudge
her awake for breakfast,
tea, even bed: *I'm coming,*
I'm not deaf. She trolls
her hands through pockets
bloated with tissue, frantic,
finding her watch (broken for years)
that *damn it, I forgot to wind.*
With quick sweetness, she
pleads for the time, fixes
the dead hands, and remembers
for an instant, exactly who she is.

FEEDING RENA

Three times a day we gather them from chairs
or corners, moving Rena last. Stuck
in permanent squat, she is a rusty jackknife
that won't open, sharp and brittle.
Her hands, cramped, unfurl into mine,
fingers cold as starving mice. I lift
her by her fists; she is breath enclosed.

Raising her arms, I pull her near dragging,
walk her to the table. Fork propped,
fierce in her hand, she weeps;
her mouth a dark nebula, gumming
dislocated narratives: *That woman is evil.*
I remind her how we eat, set the spoon
in her grip until it grafts to her palm,
move it to her lips—her eyes, stones
on a prairie road, watch everything and nothing.
Images replay in her memory's condemned
projection house—the now and the then,
flickering points, drifting in the room, stealing her.

Later, when I take her back with the others,
her vision completely unhinges;
thinking I am someone else
she mumbles a name, her face
pushing up near the boundary of a smile.
Some relived joy hums in her.
She is flesh itself seeing—the way
ecstasies still glow in ancient statues.
Her gaze tilts, fastens to the small curl
that is her body, and she asks: *What is this?*

EDITH'S SONG

She can't lift words; her tongue,
a heap against her gums, clacks
for sound. Her moaning nears
music, a priest chanting a dead
language. She is stroke-broken,
raises her eyebrows to smile,
wanting to help, floating close
when the table is set, pointing
her only arm, her slender music
teacher's finger, if you forget
a fork. She is honest somehow,
swaying beside you in a flannel
dress, as if you might ask her to
dance. At bedtime, dressing her,
you guide the flab of her stump
through the nightgown, half-
expect a hand will flower from
the sleeve to help. Her gusting
movements correct you if a button
is skipped, or a strap is too tight.
You tuck the sheets around her
and she hums a melodic outline
of words; it sounds like forgiveness.

ERNIE'S CANE

Up before the robins, shorts around his neck,
dogs next door begin to bark when he shouts:
Anyone up yet? Balanced in the hallway,
all six-five of him wanting tea, he staggers
toward you, ready to timber: *Who stole my cane?*

Hearing aid plopped out in the shag somewhere,
he's always loosing pieces of himself;
you lead him by the arm, take him back to bed,
but minutes later, he pounds his cane
on the floor, announcing: *Time for breakfast.*

One morning in socks, you step on something
moist. Ernie standing behind you, shouts:
There's my teeth, his cane punctuating the air.
I have a train at eight, he jabs. Don't disagree.
Offer tea for the road. Find the plump red pill

he refused to swallow, half-dissolved under his pillow.
Stirring its pulverized paste with sugar into the pot,
you watch as he tilts that boulder of a head to the crook
of his cane. He stares out the window, eyes beginning
to reflect the glass; his forgetting gently consumes him.

SOME THINGS I KNOW ABOUT JACK

I

He talks to you only if he likes you
and talks mostly to me.
Having learned he doesn't need to listen
he hides his hearing aid.
The staff gave up the search.

II

They found him living on the street,
brushed his hair, cleaned his suit,
called his sons. He smiles when they visit,
introducing them, beaming every time,
their forty-something cap-in-hand manners,
frayed sleeves, smell of outdoors, smiling like Jack.

III

He watches the other residents,
his secret entertainment,
sighs from a half-grin, shakes his head.
Every night setting the table—
the only one allowed to carry hot tea
or knives—he makes sure
it's safe, then lets the others sit.

IV

Jack turns the volume louder and louder
on his TV. His sons say
they found it for him.
I always knock, then turn it down.
He invites me to watch, though mostly
stares out the window,
squinting at the bright, silent world.

V

He loves the feel of a razor humming his face.
I move its coils down his cheeks
across his chin, slowly under his nose.
He rubs his skin, toothlessly whistles:
Yer aw'right, and nudges my arm.
I shout, wanting to ask how it is with him.
He gives up easily, waves me away.
I knock the old whiskers from the blades.

NANCY LEAVING

She can't keep still and rises from the table like someone in need
of cigarettes or a mother slipping to the kitchen for salt or a cloth
to wipe up thinking everyone can be satisfied trying to catch her
breath believing there's someplace to be—*thank you I really must
be going*—her mind pumping as she wobbles on flesh-starved
legs—*my husband is waiting*—her arms blue from falls and the
ground a narrow beam beneath her as our hands group like fish to
catch her then lead her back to the table—*your husband died years
ago, Nancy.* And she rises again with unfinished plates asking—
where is the kitchen—always wanting to wash-up and Jo her friend
(who doesn't know it) rises holding Nancy's hand—*this nice lady
needs to go somewhere*—leading her from breakfast dinner TV bed
anywhere leaving arm in arm searching for months down hallways
for a door that leads to a cab a bus a train waiting just outside she's
sure of it to take her home again. And Nancy loves to tell us about
teaching in Paris with her husband and if you ask she translates
the objects in the room though some words can't be found until
she thinks it's time to go and she thanks us for tea apologizing
uncertain she has money for the bill and someone rises with her for
a walk through the halls until she forgets the name of her husband.
One day I find her fallen inches from the kitchen her face cut
and swollen the damp of a fever flooding her as she weeps—*ou
est mon enfant*—carrying her to bed we change her clothes tuck
the sheets so tight she can't move and for a week she speaks only
French asking for the door and her son who flies in long enough
to see the bruise that won't heal spread like a hand over her face
while Jo hovers asking—*when will they take this nice lady home.*

VIOLET

Her silence is medieval. Her body,
a soft stone, won't stand. Lift her,
and her grey head bows to fever,
her lungs weak, her mind floods
with confusion. Raised, she walks
beside you in pilgrimage; you stop,
she stops, waits. She wants to lead
you someplace holier. Her quiet
vow, a secret dropped on the way.
Words she spoke will remain here.
Take her to her bed for the last time.
Her blue garments fall like petals.
Sponge her too-smooth arms, her legs,
crooked feet, her powder-white back.
After three days, a doctor's rushed
visit, and your quick trips between
chores, bringing soft food, she dies.
You are the last one to say her name.

ACKNOWLEDGEMENTS

Thanks to Gaspereau Press, and especially to Andrew Steeves for his finely-tuned editorial advice. I wish to acknowledge the support of the Canada Council for the Arts, the Ontario Arts Council, and the City of Ottawa Arts Funding program. Their financial assistance allowed much needed time to complete this book. Some of these poems appeared in the chapbook *Naming the Animals,* published by Rubicon Press, and also in the following journals: *The Antigonish Review, Arc Poetry Magazine, Croonenbergh's Fly, Event, The Fiddlehead, Grain, The Malahat Review, The Minnesota Review, Ottawater, Our Times, Prism International, Prairie Fire, Quills,* and *Vintage 99.* Thanks to Tim Lilburn and Lorna Crozier for encouragement and poetic sustenance early in the journey, and to Don McKay for first convincing me that a sheaf of poems could be a book. I am grateful to Jacqueline Bell for offering suggestions on many of these poems through an engaging correspondence, and to Anita Lahey for friendship and valuable feedback on earlier versions of the manuscript (and for last minute e-mails). Thanks to P. Daddie Duke Saurette for friendship, enthusiasm and the use of his cottage, and to Hank Goodfellow for just being Hank. Many of these poems passed under the careful eyes of a dedicated group of Ottawa poets who gather monthly at Mother Tongue books: thank you. Also to my colleagues at the Ottawa Public Library for understanding: merci. Thanks to the Saskatchewan Writers' Guild, their writers' colony, and to St. Peter's, where many of these poems were written. Thanks to my parents for encouragement and for showing me how to pay attention to the world. And thank you to Jacquie, my partner and companion, for your support and belief.

ALPHABETICAL LIST OF TITLES

Typeset in Fournier by Andrew Steeves & printed & bound
at Gaspereau Press under the direction of Gary Dunfield.

1   3   5   7   6   4   2

Library & Archives Canada Cataloguing in Publication

Tyler, Paul, 1969–
A short history of forgetting / Paul Tyler.

Poems.
ISBN 978-1-55447-084-6

I. Title.

PS8639.Y54S46 2010   C811'.6   C2010-901222-4

❖

GASPEREAU PRESS LIMITED
Gary Dunfield & Andrew Steeves ¶ Printers & Publishers
47 Church Avenue, Kentville, NS, Canada B4N 2M7
www.gaspereau.com